I was constantly impressed by a sense of voice, and a wonderful voice, clear and absolutely achieved. 'Oh Asda' is one of my favourites: a perfectly pitched, hilarious and disturbingly accurate picture of the way we live. Throughout *The Night My Sister Went to Hollywood*, domestic imagery makes of the kitchen and the household tasks a contemporary epic. The deceptively trivial detail of our daily lives works just as in Dickens, a great collector of trivia, and the pre-Raphaelites, revealing a powerful gift for metaphor. As Coleridge said, metaphor is an important gift of the true poet, and Hilda Sheehan has that gift in abundance.

William Bedford,
author of *Collecting Bottle Tops: Selected Poetry 1960–2008*

Hilda Sheehan uses the detail of everyday life in extraordinary juxtapositions and striking images to write about damaged relationships, dysfunctional families and a sense of displacement. Here is a poet not afraid to take risks. She often employs the surreal and breaks up syntax in a way which aptly reflects her subject matter. Behind the drama, the irony and touches of humour there is poignancy and often a huge sense of pain. A very original voice is emerging in this remarkable debut collection.

Myra Schneider,
author of *Circling the Core*
and *What Women Want*

Hilda Sheehan's poems bristle with the stuff of life, especially a woman's life. She is an Anna Wickham for the twenty-first century. She says things that help us lament, see, and celebrate what's both tricky and best in life!

Matt Holland, Director of the
Swindon Festival of Literature

It's one thing to have a vivid imagination. It's another to be adept at language. It's quite another to be gifted with the language to release and express that imagination. Hilda Sheehan has all three. She has the ability to see the pathos – as well as the joie de vivre – in the human comedy, and to convey it in a vigorous and sometimes seductively surreal language. We are enabled to see what we may not have been able or prepared to see, or even thought of seeing: this is what poetry is all about.

Robert Vas Dias,
author of *Still Life* and *Shearsman*

A joyful, freewheeling poetry that showcases a surreal wit worn with a lightness that can only be achieved through a firm grip on her craft and a sure habitation of her magically real neighbourhood. This is a collection that licks its hanky and scrubs the muck from your chops.

Martin Malone,
author of *The Waiting Hillside* and *Templar*

Hilda Sheehan's trajectory from raw talent to accomplished craftswoman has been breath-taking. Her poems are unsettling, dark, humorous and poignant at once. She has the astonishing ability to be poignant at her most bizarre and humorous. Hilda's is a risky poetry that reveals uncomfortable subtexts to do with mothering, family relationships, relationships between women, marriage and sex. This is a poet who can use bizarre, even surreal, imagery, to clarify the natural. It is a poetry to be reckoned with, a poetry deserving of a wider audience and altogether ready to be shared.

Wendy Klein,
author of *Anything in Turquoise*

Hilda Sheehan was born in 1967 in High Wycombe, Buckinghamshire and grew up in Leyland, Lancashire. She has studied English Literature and Creative Writing at the Open University, while raising five children in Swindon. She lived in Thailand for ten years, and has been a psychiatric nurse and Montessori teacher. She is editor of *Domestic Cherry* magazine and also works for Swindon Artswords (Literature Development) and the Swindon Festival of Poetry.

The Night My Sister Went to Hollywood

The Night My Sister Went to Hollywood

Hilda Sheehan

Cultured Llama Publishing

First published in 2013 by
Cultured Llama Publishing
11 London Road
Teynham, Sittingbourne
ME9 9QW
www.culturedllama.co.uk

ISBN 978-0-9568921-8-8

Printed in Great Britain by Lightning Source UK Ltd

Cover design by Mark Holihan
Front cover image copyright Jill Carter
Back cover author photo by Jaime Bullock

Contents

for Mike

Jo: I feel like throwing myself in the river.
Geoffrey: I wouldn't do that, it's full of rubbish.

A Taste of Honey, 1961

ONE

I set forth one misted white day of June
Beneath the great Atlantic rainway, and heard:
'Honestly you smite worlds of truth, but
Lose your own trains of thought, like a pigeon.'

'And that is the modern idea of fittingness,
To, always in motion, lose nothing, although beneath the
Rainway they move in threes and twos completely
Ruined by themselves, like moving pictures.'

— Kenneth Koch, from 'On the Great Atlantic Rainway'

Stella: He smashed all the light bulbs with the heel
of my slipper.
Blanche DuBois: And you let him? Didn't run,
didn't scream?
Stella: Actually, I was sorta thrilled by it.

— *A Streetcar Named Desire,* 1951

Not in the Stars

I was never a Vivien Leigh
but we rode the same streetcar once:
her on the way to torment,
me on the way back.

She said she was written by men
and not in the stars:
disgusting, filthy, greasy men that lie
and dislike noisy women.

'I've never lied in my heart,' she cried.

How morbid, I thought, as we transferred
to a streetcar named *Cemetery*
then rode six blocks to Elysian Fields
where she got off, bright as a naked light bulb,
left me in the empty streetcar
to throb with exciting life.

Don't Tell Louise

Jesus is the man driving us to the Co-op
for bread. He asks, 'are either of you cold?'
I raise my hand, he turns up the heat.

Louise says, 'he's fake: no one can walk on water,
no one can rise from the dead.'
But I'm not so sure, Jesus is perfectly nice,

he offers us eternal life, 'Believe in me,
I'll turn left at the lights into heaven,
honestly.' I smile,

when he talks about our father, how he plants
tomatoes: he's good to the earth
but not to any of us.

'That's God', he says. 'Don't expect so much.'
Then it goes quiet, all of us looking out
of one window or another,

until Louise whispers, 'Christ! let's do a runner
when he stops, the guy's nuts. We'll get dressed up,
put on make-up, do our hair, paint our nails.'

Later, in a club some lads buy us drinks,
they want to take us home. I think of Jesus,
but don't tell Louise.

The Seal

Sometimes,
the seal from next door borrows my bathtub
to loll in cool water. He says, 'there's nowhere left
to get wet,' and lets himself in with the key I leave
in a dried up sea under broken corrugated coral.

When I get home,
I close the mouth of the loo; sit and watch
him swish this way and that; his fat, wet behind
rises up and down like a barren island in a storm,
sending waves to me –

the kind that make you want to club the wicked,

or throw a fish.

Later,
when only his head can be seen,
we talk in ripples that circle him;
silence our lost worlds.

I don't know why he comes, it's not as if we're lovers:
he's a seal, and I just live here.

Nudibranch

were they floral
there would be songs for
sea-slugs too
Choisui 1813, translation Robin D. Gill

If he could see me now: dribbling
like a sea-slug –

a shell-less regal goddess
dreaming of him

in naked, soft-bodied,
sea-going sleep.

If he could see me now
the way I sleep:

over-washed flannel pyjamas,
buttons missing,

old knickers, toxic breath –
the dribbling –

he wouldn't thank me
for these kisses we share:

jelly-body, rubbed by waves –
a sea-slug dreaming of him

at the bottom of my shallow
love-resistant bed.

A Tragedy from a Bathtub

I'd listen to my father recite Shakespeare
from his bathtub, my ear
to the bathroom door.
He was my jewel set in a silver sea,
my mighty Caesar.

Our mother, Juliet, would be downstairs
washing up the breakfast things
dreaming of Romeo,
her lover, mowing our lawn,
cutting tree branches dagger sharp.

One day, after my father's bath,
he found the washing-up had not been done;
it sat in the swamp of the sink,
mourning for my mother
who was found on the lawn,
presumed dead.
Romeo was with her, speared dead
by the branch of a tree.

When mother awoke,
she tackled the washing up,
but found life too dull without Romeo
and left, through a door
I could never find in the cellar.

I'd listen to my father recite Wordsworth,
for he believed no harm could come of daffodils.
And I was lonely as the cloud he lay on
while our washing up grew
into a crockery mountain.

Dragoljub Obnažena!

Me and Dragoljub sit in the bathtub u uživanju.
Our small lake sings daleko but he thinks in guitar.
Let's go to Japanski he says i utiskuje large feet
between my breasts – moja strast!
I turn taps to zadivljujući hot, o radosti.
But he's neoprezna ponekad with my feelings
such spoilt bubbles, he's polako made instinski
silna and I am obnažena! Oh kako sam žude
for warm dry towels of savršenstvom.

Mermaid

Like a mermaid washed up on the sheets
she lifts two silver ballet-stockinged feet
until the cockle of her weedy pouch
protrudes and urges him to touch –
drink silver, slippery fishes
of their night.

Dressed hoary-blue waiting for her mirror,
hidden in his jacket for all tomorrows –
he's frightened that his love will disappear,
downstairs lost, brown and dreary,
in her sea of washing up
and life.

The Golden Lampstand

Men: We've come for the lampstand.
Woman: I'm using it right now. You'll have to come back later.
Men: God wants it now.
Woman: God will have to wait.
I am writing a poem and I need the light
of that particular lamp.
Men: Look! He is coming with the clouds.
Woman: I am coming with a poem.
Men: He has a loud voice like a trumpet.
Woman: I have a poem loud like a lion
that can destroy the earth.

Flashes of lightning followed by a severe hailstorm.

Men: Look what you have done.
Woman: It's just a poem, a poem done on the edge
of a filthy sink. I'm sorry for my mistakes but I do not have
the time to correct them.
Men: Just give us the golden lampstand and repent.
Woman: When I've finished cooking this poem.

The poem begins to smoke. Out of the smoke comes a cloud of locusts with the faces of men who are serious about poetry.

Men: Your poem is neither cold nor hot.
Woman: It is trying to be one or the other. It does not want
to be lukewarm.
Men: Cover your shameful poems. Put them on the fire
and give us the lampstand.
Woman: My poem is wearing white, it is not naked.
Although underneath it is very naked.
Men: We know your poem. It is probably homely.

Woman: It has a sword in its mouth.

Men: Everybody will suffer from this poem. It is at the point of death and speaks in Balak.

Woman: It is riding a beast and only eats manna.

Men: It is Jezebel!

Woman: It has so-called deep secrets.

Men: It has soiled its clothes and refuses to be dressed in white or credible punctuation.

Woman: It is for whoever has ears that can never be shut.

The woman shuts the door and all the locusts with the faces of men eat the men at the door.

Kitchen Drama

So many women in one kitchen:
cleaning the sides, scrubbing the oven.
They set the timer for hours and hours
of the same, 24, 24, then set it again.

Martha cries, she will never get another load in
before midnight, and it spins
her head into creases –
there's not an inch of kitchen
without a woman moving on it,
there's colour and white, fights over
Persil and Bold 3.
Mary sobs for comfort.

As for cooking, Lydia has started to mash
and Anna to stew: they will mash and stew
until Tuesday, when something gets boiled.

The moon is a bowl of sugar.

Rebecca becomes the shape of kitchen,
her brain fills the sink.
She notices her face gone
to tough kitchen-paint, fully scrubbable.

Hannah pours soup for a thousand children,
warms a wooden spoon on the quiet of her dress,
leans her hair into dripping, then leaves,
to drive a car (someone has to move the corpse).

The others get distorted, excited on bleach,
explode into dragonflies,
tremble for cooking oil as dishcloths drip
from the ceiling like pupas.

There's an empty cupboard
where the crying started.
Martha wonders when the floors will get done.

The Woman who Licked Ice

2012 had been a bad year
for June,
she started eating ice, every day

a jug full. This distracted her
from pain,
freezing fog, thick rime.

Her family thought it weird:
sneaking
to the shed eating ice,

a strange habit! So she took
one final piece;
the biggest crystal in the bag,

licked it instead, to make it last
longer –
amazed licking gave such satisfaction:

this was good ice, ancient glacier ice,
Isklar ice!
and 'Oh Ginnungagap!' she cried.

But no one understood, not licks
nor language
happening in her mouth.

Ice thoughts came in licks,
this rock
lasted days – and with the licking,

an eye suddenly appeared.
She licked
some more: licked hairy chest,

licked thigh, licked toe, licked tongue
'til tongue
licked back and out of nothingness

a man appeared from the ice!
'A man!'
she declared. 'How magical! How lovely!

Oh Ginnungagap!'

Slices

Bread began to slice the woman.
'Don't slice me,' cried the woman,

but bread had no mercy for women:
sliced woman is delicious
with husbands and children on top, thought bread –

it smelt her rising in the warmth
of a loaf: made neat, white, and bad
for the heart when buttered by knives.

Some of her was stored in a man-tin for the next day.
Bread wondered how one little woman
could create such crumbs.

Spring Dinner

It is spring. I serve my children up
a plate of violets, primroses
bluebells on a side dish
and they cry that their mother is mad.

'Where is the usual meat?'
'Where are the potatoes?'
'Where is the real food?'

I repeat the birdsong of the garden.
Blossom comes down in the wind.

For pudding, I serve late snow,
snow that cries out of them colder

the next day.

I fold their napkin faces into wings
that fly back to winter.

The Last Time We Made Cake

a pint of hot tea could hear
the milking of our ears.

3 ounces of soft Demerara
raised the wholemeal out of flour,

made ½ of myself twice.

I was once 1 teaspoon
of mixed spice and a large egg.

Some said soak the fruit in tea,
cover and leave overnight,

but that's plain neglect.

Set at gas mark 7
you pre-heated us to burn,

we tried to talk about it –
winced when fruit

kept coming in as liquid

and I became a soft
dropping consistency

fairly low in the oven
till risen and firm.

Longwave

From London to Luxembourg –
those longwave angry voices
downstairs –
your father shouts,
'Turn that thing off!
It says too much in song –

sharp
            distant
                        terrible.'

Your mother's corpse is laid out
on a broken aerial;
she signals daytime programmes
at the turn of a knob;
a bus crashes through on treble;
seventeen dead and more to come
at tea time's lonely ache
for suffering and sleep

as the news of someone's daughter
is washed up on the beach.

Earth Time 2673/Ship Time 1972

Let him not breed in great numbers, for he will make a desert of his home and yours.
Planet of the Apes, 1968

Back when men smoked cigars on spaceships and women were strapped in first, 700 years on board and everyone on Earth dead, we had to float for our lives on wallpaper patterns of false brick and out of control leaves. It was a question of survival: the fucked-up were having kids – *lots of love-making but no love.* We cannot blame the wallpaper, the spaceships or the smoking … it was 1972/2673 and *Planet of the Apes* made perfect sense to all of us, it was everything we'd hoped for since 1968: Kim Hunter, such a pretty and homely ape.

Jemima World

The hell, goddammit, that's not supposed to happen!
Westworld, 1973

for Michael Scott

His choice was beautiful but she couldn't stop talking robot, not to him and all the other seekers in the park. Even when she was undressing there was so much to be said. 'You talk too much,' he shouted, and shut her away in a cupboard, naked, then called for help. Customer services said there was a computer malfunction and that someone would be with him shortly. 'Sit tight, watch some telly and we'll make arrangements for you to take a hovercraft to Cynthia World where *desire ends in satisfaction.* Cynthia is mute.' But all he could hear was this naked robot jabbering away in in the wardrobe: 'I said you talk too much!' Next time, he'll bring the wife.

Ekky Delph

They found our neighbour,
dead last week, in Ekky Delph,
it was in the paper.

My mother said, 'he's just a torso:
no arms, no legs, no head,'
while eating toast.

'I wonder where
they put the rest of him.'

My father stared
and looked out of the window.
The police were bringing out
what looked like body pieces in bin bags.

'Do you think his wife's alive?' he asked.
'No woman could manage that.'

But I had seen her drive away one night;
eyes on full beam – hair like wild fire

and I wondered if she might.

In the Ballroom

Blackpool, 1979,

she's in her best hair,
          tight dress,
                    shiny shoes.

He's been dancing her
          for thirty years –

     a regimented tango.

She thinks of Eugenio

on a Friday night – his Argentine cha cha cha!

a body

     strong enough

               to drop her

catch her again

          before she dies.

Man, Woman, Tap, Baby, Duck

i
Squeezy-bottle, bleach, a thought:
I am a stamp
edible but plain –
an envelope
keeps my body woken,
nothing of the think left:

wasn't it you who licked me down?

Rotten housewives empty the wind of their own snow,
bomb the created,
slaughter honey-suckle, sheared –
buds of dead
show life
on the path that way (taps left running).

ii
The duck is broken
all mended
and flying. Who killed it?
Who gave the life to a duck
          killed?
Let's fly ourselves unwanted:
how can the upgraded flyer
walk?

A need for duck, brick and sofa
beneath it
above the floor is where
to keep the things
the neighbours said.

iii
Up on the wall a string
of men
held
by their very own socks.
How hard it is to blow
them easily; what a fall
of men
it might be if we can't keep them
        like this
on the kitchen windowsill:
basil plant, wooden spoon, broken pot
        separate and hide
all together
                one day cleared away
into what? A man? Comes with his truck
collects, sells to a new woman
buys the old
other women ever
wanted, so, clean up Mrs. Hughes said
man, woman, tap, baby, duck.

The Space Between Two Windows

from the outside could be hallway,
junk cupboard, secret passage, top of stairs,

a place for the lonely chair,
or a telephone to ring,

where flowers die slowly in a vase
on top of an occasional table,

and fingers of light creep out
from other people's rooms,

a place to frame a holiday
and nail it on the wall –

the space between two windows
with no view at all.

The House that Died

One day, our house stopped breathing.
A passer-by noticed it going blue
as noise escaped from an open window:
there was a gasp, a choke.

People came out –
patted it on the back, made suggestions:

Cut the hedge down, tidy the garden,
weed it, scrape it, paint it a brilliant white –
don't walk on the grass for God's sake!

Punch it in the chest, electrocute it, stick
a knife in its throat – insert a straw, then blow.

Nothing helped.
The council pronounced it dead
in its corner plot:
It just gave up the will to be a home.

How it suffered – tried so hard to breathe,
make space, be tidy, stylish, organised –
look nice like other houses on the street.

It went stiff and black quite quickly;
flesh fell from its frame,
like bricks toppling from a tall building.

In the silence of our grief,
we chased flies off its back,
left the bones for a viewing,
no funeral though.

Oh Asda!

1
Look how we dream in home delivery,
all dolled up George
buying our hearts out,

smart priced and mad, tired mothers,
down dull isles of clueless product,
the suffering wives:

suppressed, stacked baskets,
gagged by dusters sold on shelf 13.
We feed our young expired values,

left cold in the fridge for days –
look closer: see the vulgar stamps
on eggs, our toxic guilty plastics.

Let's roll it back girls:
those pork-chop love aisles
are three for ten pounds –

can we afford to buy?

2
Gail works the self-checkout
dead by the end of the day
in *card not accepted.*

Check the age of a gaunt neglected child
buying vodka:
drunk useless teen sickness

in a bag for life grows numb,
knowing no one,
not even man, can face this trauma.

Gail returns the baskets, bins
forsaken receipts,
takes home some fags and

a bottle of wine for mum.

3
A child screams
in Smarties colour vomit,
vegetables

are putrid ghosts
a mother used to buy,
cook to death.

The smacked child screams more,
dragged away from sweet desire,
milk teeth aching,

yellow tongue sour on mummy
as he shows her
his insides already unhealthy,

brain cells jump jelly bean-high,
he's strapped
in the trolley –

why won't he sit still?

You Said That I Could Write to You

when it's quiet, when I'm feeding the twins.
I'm feeding the twins spaghetti and sausages,

it is not healthy. I have spaghetti
in my brain, up my nose.

Those sausages look like fingers
trying to write.

Forgive this page of stains:
poo, crying, dirty washing, lack of sleep.

The windows are covered
with fingerprints,

and I'm surrounded by maps
of places I would like to go.

Where are the doors?
Where is the path?

I've always wanted to ask:
what was it like,

to carry your daughters around
with all those poems?

What kind of a mother writes poems
anyway, and why?

I don't know when I can send this,
the post office is not on the map

and stamps are heavy, aren't they?

The Night My Sister Went to Hollywood

she left a stare on the bathroom mirror
and rubber gloves slumped over taps
like yellow dresses waiting for a clean.

There was a smashing of plates after tea
to avoid washing-up and what she cooked
for the kids before she left

could not be saved – not the fish
that wasted itself for years just swimming
nor the bacon that never met bread.

One earring left behind was mistaken
for the one she took with her; unique
and beautiful, hooked on the scent of pillow.

Hollywood made a film with most of the crying
included, ending with the hope of highlights,
Botox, bigger lips and no one seemed to care

if her bed was made, if her bed was unmade.

TWO

Most people want a man! So here I am
I have a pheasant in my reminders I have a goshawk in my clouds
Whatever is it which has led all these animals to you?

— Kenneth Koch, from 'Alive for an instant'

James Duncan: Find me the architect that designed you, and who needs Doug Roberts?
Susan: I do.

— *The Towering Inferno,* 1974

The Towering Inferno

The place was burning down
and we were not able to use the lift
because of an upturned wheelbarrow of cement
blocking the door,
we were at the very top
where firemen could not reach us
(this was in the sky and nearly to space)
and one of them said,
one of these days you're gonna kill 10,000
in one of these firetraps,
and the selfish men tried to get out first,
on a chair,
on a wire to another building,
leaving behind their high-heeled women
by the buffet,
and we were left to burn like lovers in a bed –
until you ran for help with a wet towel over your head,
through fire and more fire,
while smoke came in under the door,
I dreamed of Robert Vaughn
because *all fires are bad,*
I fell, a burning ball from a window
and you were not there to watch.
In the end they laid out all the dead: there was you,
and there was me –
we were one building I figured would never burn.

Stuffing

I'd take bits of you home with me –
something from your pocket, or a piece
of soft stuffing from the ripped quilting
of your parka, while our hoods overlapped:
no talking, just kissing
for hours in the cold and rain.

It would live in my hand or by my pillow,
smelling of your body and those dreams
that took off where our doorstep kisses
left us: on the floor in my hallway,
a hot radiator steaming us dry
as we rolled out naked –
until the light shone through on your face:
when you remember the last quick kiss,
you alone whispering goodnight
to a slammed door, then kicking
pebbles home, singing *Love Action*,
scuffing your shoes, wishing we were older.

The Long Walk Home

He wanted to take me away, to Leicester,
Grimsby, Preston; take my pick, decide later.

Come on, think about it – Skegness, Coventry?
We can get jobs or buy an ice cream van,

close up whenever we wanted to kiss
over cones under swirls of Mr Whippy, Rockets –

just one Cornetto and a Screwball dearest.
Instead, I got off home, did the kids' tea,

the shopping, made the beds, polished the TV,
washed up, hoovered, fed the cat.

I'd touched his cheek; he'd softened, dripped
to my feet. I thought of those long hot summer walks

home from school with an ice-cream melted
before I could eat it, thinking: *what a waste.*

Your Eyes Are Nearly Your Best Feature

but, your belly is like East Anglia;
I can see all the way down long legs out to sea.

Your breasts: the Pennines, or should I say Peaks?
Papplewick Pump Station!

I could eat off you; such a clean,
lovely thing to lick the pattern off: Palissy,

Shelly Blue Empress, Queen Anne –
made in the pug mill, carried to the potter.

How can I possess you? Island with trees
that cover the isolated parts of me.

If I climb, look from your highest point,
I'm sure there's an unusual light.

beautiful is told a thing or two

1
beautiful I'll wait for you until the clock strikes beautiful
at midnight and one

2
beautiful all we want is jewel-lipped laughter glossed
away why wasn't your father told

3
beautiful I want to lay beside you take my small tongs
curl your hair to swans

4
beautiful something tells me the gate was locked behind
you forever lights left singing

5
beautiful I'll buy your children the things of gold shops
dug up treasure why not take them

6
beautiful we must make a cloudburst make a river
make a whole mountain climb up between

7
beautiful I will alter you up like a god like sweet things
gifted dressed to stop the world beautiful

8
beautiful I told you each day will always be
a beautiful place to picnic in your perfume

9
beautiful I will hang you up above a shelf of things
that describe your face my wall loves you too

10
beautiful if you go down the shops the ugly
might buy you with biscuits a paper a coffee

Avebury Stone Man

for Martin Malone

It took 5,000 years to make this man;
he's earthwork, chalk and ditch,
time and weather.

I see you on his hill – a monument
compared to his ground-down shape:
tall, slender, of stone yourself.

You ask me, 'who would build a road
through the middle of this?'
as if you were made

when these stones were made,
and I think of the spring,
when waters fill and make

the shape of a Goddess –
raising these cold stones in pairs,
as ley lines kiss, your

chalk-land magnetism calling.

My Lover Searches for a Stick of Rock to Bring Back from the Seaside

It's been years since I sucked
letters down to a slim white sugar stick,

wrapped the last inch back up
and pocketed the sticky.

When I found it, later,
I remembered the words you wrote

through me in red smudge streaks;

wrapped, beautiful but stuck, irresistible,
took my teeth around the journey

to a bright, unforgettable bite.

Various Things

after Kenneth Koch

I love you, I do. It's just that,
time is running out, it's Sunday. Asda will shut soon.
Do we need rice? Cinnamon?
Look up there, where the bird used to be. Concorde!
With this, we could make a wonderful child.
Will you run me up the road?
Heaven knows, I'm miserable, now,
please put the bins out.
Remember Holborn? When you kissed me,
a train stopped and let more people on.
I love the red bits in your hair.
Shall we dust?
If you move next door, we could pretend to be lovers.
When you get back, we could put up a shelf.
You make me want to jump off a cliff.
Let's make cheese toasties in the Breville.
In a past life, I was a daffodil.
Why did you pick me?
1987. U2? With or without you,
getting high on the smell of your John Player Blues.

(0,0)

She knew nothing of maths
but her love insisted,
(he with his $z = x^2 - y^2$ head on)
that if all second partial derivatives
of *she* exist, then the Hessian matrix
of *he* is the matrix and indefinite.
'We are a two-player zero sum:
one positive, one negative
real eiginvalue.
Us = the point (0,0)
and I love you has no sum at all
which is a complicated problem.'

Six Tips for Love

1

Get to the point. Release your actual story right away.
No-one is interested until they know what your story is.

2

Include a human. You must be real. Then, she can speak
to you.

3

Think: madder, sadder, richer, poorer people than you
find love without too many statistics and facts.

4

The weight of buses carries more love on a daily basis
than numbers of people in football stadiums (who are all
thinking of love).

5

In short, one paragraph is plenty: I was born, I am the
son of a shoemaker, but I work in McDonalds – get her
attention – the need to know.

6

And finally, draw your mobile number in the sky, in
case she has forgotten by the morning that you ever left
yourself behind.

My Man in McDonalds

smells of cheeseburger and chips. A McFlurry
taste tips his tongue; he's salt splashed.

He controls ten tills lost to teenagers,
teatime mums: counter to door-deep cravers.

I too crave his same old, same old kiss –
chicken nugget lips in a dip of curry.

Coffee for Two

for Mike

See how the cappuccinos
hold our sugar –

       suspended sweetness
       on a bed of milky froth

until it falls into that hot blind blur
that keeps us up all night.

Wooden Cow

'What the heck am I supposed to do
with that?' she said,
folding her arms, looking disgusted.

She wanted a new gold ring,
chocolates, designer clothes –
was spoilt rotten.

His intentions were good: a man
who thought he understood
a woman's need for bull,

so he pulled over the cowhide:
patted her inside
for a bit of unnatural love.

Cleaning

Thoughts of you
fall down
the kitchen sink,
are washed and bleached
out of existence,
or dried up
into small
white side plates.
You are vacuumed;
sucked and binned,
smeared on windows
then vigorously
wiped way.
At the end of the day
when all is tidy
I press you, press you
into neat
starched squares
that I fold
and put in a drawer
somewhere –
I know I put you somewhere.

where all the kisses that ever happened to us

speak in violet   wild rose   fairy flavours

smooth as love running smooth

roars you   the saddest tale

of harmonious rude seas

sings *meet my moonlight*

cowslip ear   cowslip tall

a freckle storm   on a summer's day

to hang a pearl   on a fruitless star

where all the kisses

that ever happened to us join in bright confusion

spread themselves   real as any dream

Sundance

'Let's go to Manchester,' you said.
'I've never been to Manchester.'
And while the world became civilised, we did,
through a hole-in-the-wall,
a small price to pay for beauty,
and I had all the ideas and you were all action
and skill, sheer luck it was
that Manchester was open at that time
of our lives, that we could escape.
It was then that you broke the news, 'Hilda,'
you said, 'there's something I ought to tell you.
I never loved anybody before.'

'One hell of a time to tell me,' I said.

Marcia

Sat in the day room, Marcia looks up at me,
her burnt face scarred tight to no expression –

'I fed it to the gas cooker,' she spoke.
Lucky to be alive, I think out loud –

she disagrees, doesn't know why
she's still sitting there on tablets and ECT.

'It's an illness: the need to burn a pretty face,'
said Doctor Fred in last week's ward round

(he likes first name terms; gets him closer
to his patients, without getting close).

I sit down, look but don't look.
I know about the knife

she keeps with her vests, the tablets
saved in life-saving batches are sick

and slightly dissolved, they've already been
to damp places of small white plastic cups.

There are times when the unthinkable
roars out of me too, 'Marcia,'

I say, 'fancy Scrabble?'

Gordon

teaches me about clothes –
what cloth and body speak
to goodnight men
in bus stations.

Twenty quid will screw
the markings of a wrist –
body out and bargained
uncovered hips

the suck and spit
at bus-door-shadows.

Off to sleep for (close to)
two and half
in old jersey pants
white t-shirt

shoes wet and broke.

Eating is in pieces –
jam sick mornings,
mugs of, plates of
(ah or uh).

Come daylight
come buses
come men
back in jobs

thoughts became blouses:
cotton neat, scented
clears out
what was worn the night before

the night before.

Pink 'N' Whites

You run in your sleep, need a bigger bed,
like the one in the Sheraton.

You have nightmares, cry for the violin
in the Ashmolean; all your unplayed

unborn poems that fall apart
on days when only Pink 'N' Whites

suffice, because food is complicated
and so is life.

You can talk for hours
in astonishing floods, sugar mouth

layers of sweet shock,
'this actually happened,' you say, 'to me.'

In this car, we turn a corner,
speak of happy camels and God

and you tell me, after six more Pink 'N' Whites
that you always fall asleep in cars:

'be careful,' you say to the sleeping you
in there, 'dreams have teeth.'

Pink 'N' Whites are mallow biscuits made by Caxton

Dan

Dan walked my way home,
had black teeth and fleas,
told me he saw a flasher once,
I said it was probably God
trying to tell him something:
to get out more, to do well at school.

Dan fell,
grazed the side of his face bad.
I cleaned it with a dock leaf,
spit and tissue; I could smell
school, dog and piss on him.

He followed me
for weeks after that,
waited one Saturday
for me to rise, draw my curtains.
I went down, asked him
if he had a home, a mother,
anything?

Then he kissed me,
a kiss that crippled me,
folded my spine,
sucked out my heart.

I heard he jumped
from twenty floors,
bones like pick-up sticks.

Ugly

The unattractive woman will never be:
not the size of her breasts, nor her not
pout, nor an hour glass
goes by at the lack of smile
as she tuts the kitchen tight a fuck it.

Please kettle on and broom handle,
please suck out your ugly in cans
of fish mouth defying ugly –

greet the postman a heaven waits stamp,

sulk, stomp, cry!

What the God did you wake for?
How mountains did you buy that dress?
The cost of you is ugly inside out.
You think all day a diet weight scoff.

Ugly in the kitchen,
ugly on the bus,
ugly by the roadside,
ugly in concrete,
ugly mother cries in smacks,
ugly of Britain,
ugly sitting ugly,

aren't we all?

The Parting

He was an old bloke. Not a bloke
looking young for his age, or one
to hide lovers in the village
away from a kitchen wife, or make

up stories down the local pub
to a crowd of mates. He was alone;
you don't dress in green Crimplene
trousers with off-white grubby

shirt for anyone else. His parting
of coarse grey hair was the first thing
that struck me; how it split him
right down the middle: two parts,

symmetrical (half sad, half sad).
I'd a vision of him as a boy,
his mother combing him in two,
expecting he would stay like that.

Henry and Susie are Missing

i

Susie, this is the bed speaking. And a wanted moon blew broken kiss words mostly blink-spelt.

Soon an open window throws cold on the speaking bed: who is missing? Manic-squashed sheets fly east and miss-speak.

Tuesday the bed is a yellow duck fed from Henry's childhood. It gulps hate shut, all feet sink south. In scattered arms they disappear to the bottom of a sad whereabouts.

Henry and Susie are missing. Love shakes the sheets for evidence of guilt, kiss, embrace, lust and disappointed crumpled doing crumpled finds a shoe.

A cluster bomb drops sheet mess and sweet nothing surprises them asleep. Their mothers call in soup to throw the home made kitchen guilt to cook a missing couple on gas. Did Henry? Did Susie?

The missing mess is nothing. Compare a price tag lip sulk. The missing mess tidies up tights and weeps to a shirt tale that a wedding's about: a great big dress of white nasty.

Henry and Susie, describe for me the hidden danger of ironed on bliss. When did your love go missing? Did your love find out in a word?

ii

Henry: I want to take you missing in that dress. I want your slippers last night.

Susie: My slippers have no voice, never want the voiceless, here the bed speaks moon kiss. Want the bed!

Henry: My wings are brooding what is in you and dark. Are we missing or are we lost in oblivious wandering?

Susie: Here loses nothing but a happy state of fruit and wild waste. Let us stay missing longer.

Henry: We can't go missing too long: guilt, kiss, embrace, lust and disappointed throw true love on the sheets.

Susie: Quietly, we can stay missing, the neighbours think a postman murdered our mail for ink and rain junk.

Henry: Your voiceless missing envelope is stuffed through a next door hole. Glass bit the postman.

Susie: All flesh is glass. Feel my see-through self, the rain on me, the junk on me smells a paper coming in.

iii

After the missing the paper hole got bigger words on it. Henry listened to the not said each night in case Susie escaped. He invited tea and cakes more often and told the neighbours a safe thing or two about missing lovers.

The neighbours looked out. Windows wide opened a glare of don't dare. No one went missing.

Henry missed being missing. Susie lost her voice. She hid her slippers from Henry and shushed her feet say nothing.

Feet blurted the whereabouts. Susie cried voiceless screams that only played in her head: This is an unfair world where men walk first, I must step out in my own fur naked animal vest, I must be missing and scream a human loud.

Henry was home all day. The chair sat him straight. No Henry! Not that football result. Tight shut your man!

How found was what? Love was in the biscuit tin. Kiss was in a kitchen cupboard. Guilt was under something under something else. Embrace was nowhere. Embrace they thought was dead behind the fridge. Lust laid out its whole body on a rug and waited for more. Henry definitely found disappointed.

Susie sneaked out missing. Henry felt worse after letting her back in to unmiss the night she left behind. What if we came back really, never to be found?

Do you know a more missing story?

THE END

Acknowledgements

Some of these poems have been published in the following: *The Rialto, Poetry Salzburg Review, ARTEMISPoetry, South, Ariadne's Thread, Octopus* (Templar 2012), *Unexplored Territory* (Cultured Llama 2012), *The Poetry Kite, CITN* (Poetry Kit), *Ink Sweat and Tears,* the BBC website and the BBC Big Screen Swindon.

Thanks to Mike Sheehan for his unending support at home that makes it possible for me to write poems. Grateful thanks to William Bedford for his generosity and close reading of the manuscript. Thanks also to those who have encouraged, supported and helped with individual poems in this collection on various occasions over the years: Matt Holland, Michael Scott, Cristina Newton, Robert Vas Dias, Myra Schneider, Bethany Pope, Martin Malone, Carrie Etter, Wendy Klein, Jim Bennett, Daljit Nagra, Ros Barber, Alan Buckley, Mimi Khalvati, Anne-Marie Fyfe, Dr Mike Johnson and Ben Lawrence. Thank you to Maria C. McCarthy and Dr Bob Carling at Cultured Llama for their enthusiastic encouragement and for their hard work in the publication of this book.

Cultured Llama Publishing

hungry for poetry
thirsty for fiction

Cultured Llama was born in a converted stable. This creature of humble birth drank greedily from the creative source of the poets, writers, artists and musicians that visited, and soon the llama fulfilled the destiny of its given name.

Cultured Llama is a publishing house, a multi-arts events promoter and a fundraiser for charity. It aspires to quality from the first creative thought through to the finished product.

www.culturedllama.co.uk

Also published by Cultured Llama

A Radiance
by Bethany W. Pope

Paperback; 70pp; 203x127mm;
978-0-9568921-3-3; June 2012
Cultured Llama

Family stories and extraordinary images glow throughout this compelling debut collection from an award-winning author, like the disc of uranium buried in her grandfather's backyard. *A Radiance* 'gives glimpses into a world both contemporary and deeply attuned to history – the embattled history of a family, but also of the American South where the author grew up.'

'A stunning debut collection... these poems invite us to reinvent loss as a new kind of dwelling, where the infinitesimal becomes as luminous as ever.'

Menna Elfyn

'*A Radiance* weaves the voices of four generations into a rich story of family betrayal and survival, shame and grace, the visceral and sublime. A sense of offbeat wonder at everyday miracles of survival and love both fires these poems and haunts them – in a good way.'

Tiffany S. Atkinson

'An exhilarating and exceptional new voice in poetry.'

Matthew Francis

Also published by Cultured Llama

strange fruits
by Maria C. McCarthy

Paperback; 72pp; 203x127mm;
978-0-9568921-0-2; July 2011
Cultured Llama (in association with
WordAid.org.uk)

Maria is a poet of remarkable skill, whose work offers surprising glimpses into our 21st-century lives – the 'strange fruits' of our civilisation or lack of it. Shot through with meditations on the past and her heritage as 'an Irish girl, an English woman', *strange fruits* includes poems reflecting on her urban life in a Medway town and as a rural resident in Swale.

Maria writes, and occasionally teaches creative writing, in a shed at the end of her garden.

All profits from the sale of *strange fruits* go to Macmillan Cancer Support, Registered Charity Number 261017.

'Maria McCarthy writes of the poetry process: "There is a quickening early in the day" ('Raising Poems'). A quickening is certainly apparent in these humane poems, which are both natural and skilful, and combine the earthiness and mysteriousness of life. I read *strange fruits* with pleasure, surprise and a sense of recognition.'

Moniza Alvi

Also published by Cultured Llama

Canterbury Tales on a Cockcrow Morning
by Maggie Harris

Paperback; 136pp; 203x127mm;
978-0-9568921-6-4; September 2012
Cultured Llama

Maggie Harris brings warmth and humour to her *Canterbury Tales on a Cockcrow Morning*, and tops them with a twist of calypso.

Here are pilgrims old and new: Eliot living in 'This Mother Country' for half a century; Samantha learning that country life is not like in the magazines.

There are stories of regret, longing and wanting to belong; a sense of place and displacement resonates throughout.

> 'Finely tuned to dialogue and shifting registers of speech, Maggie Harris' fast-moving prose is as prismatic as the multi-layered world she evokes. Her Canterbury Tales, sharply observed, are rich with migrant collisions and collusions.'

> John Agard

Also published by Cultured Llama

The Strangest Thankyou
by Richard Thomas

Paperback; 98pp; 203x127mm;
978-0-9568921-5-7; October 2012
Cultured Llama

Richard Thomas's debut poetry collection embraces the magical and the mundane, the exotic and the everyday, the surreal rooted in reality.

Grand poetic themes of love, death and great lives are cut with surprising twists and playful use of language, shape, form and imagery.

The poet seeks 'an array of wonder' in "Dig" and spreads his 'riches' throughout *The Strangest Thankyou*.

'He has long been one to watch, and with this strong, diverse collection Richard Thomas is now one to read. And re-read.'

Matt Harvey

Also published by Cultured Llama

Unauthorised Person
by Philip Kane

Paperback; 74pp; 203x127mm;
978-0-9568921-4-0; November 2012
Cultured Llama

Philip Kane describes *Unauthorised Person* as a 'concept album' of individual poems, sequences, and visuals, threaded together by the central motif of the River Medway.

This collection draws together poems written and images collected over 27 years, exploring the psychogeography of the people and urban landscapes of the Medway Towns, where 'chatham high street is paradise enough' ("johnnie writes a quatrain").

'This collection shows a poet whose work has grown in stature to become strong, honest and mature. Yet another voice has emerged from the Medway region that I'm sure will be heard beyond our borders. The pieces here vary in tone, often lyrical, sometimes prosaic but all show a deep rooted humanity and a political (with a small p) sensibility.'

Bill Lewis

Unexplored Territory
edited by Maria C. McCarthy

Paperback; 112pp; 203x127mm;
978-0-9568921-7-1; November 2012
Cultured Llama

Unexplored Territory is the first anthology from
Cultured Llama – poetry and fiction that take a
slantwise look at worlds, both real and imagined.

'A dynamic range of new work by both established and
emerging writers, this anthology offers numerous delights.

The themes and preoccupations are wide-ranging. Rooted
in close observation, the poems and short fiction concern the
'unexplored territory' of person and place.

A must for anyone who likes good writing.'

Nancy Gaffield
author of *Tokaido Road*

Contributors:

Jenny Cross
Maggie Drury
June English
Maggie Harris
Mark Holihan
Sarah Jenkin

Philip Kane
Luigi Marchini
Maria C. McCarthy
Rosemary McLeish
Gillian Moyes
Bethany W. Pope

Hilda Sheehan
Fiona Sinclair
Jane Stemp
Richard Thomas
Vicky Wilson

Lightning Source UK Ltd.
Milton Keynes UK
UKOW031345200213

206507UK00007B/289/P